Guys and Guns Amok

ALSO BY DOUGLAS KELLNER

Herbert Marcuse: Art and Liberation, edited (2007)

Media Spectacle and the Crisis of Democracy: Terrorism, War, and Election Battles (2005)

Herbert Marcuse and the New Left, edited (2004)

Fredric Jameson: A Critical Reader, coedited with Sean Homer (2004)

From 9/11 to Terror War: The Dangers of the Bush Legacy (2003)

Media Spectacle (2003)

Grand Theft 2000: Media Spectacle and a Stolen Election (2001)

The Postmodern Adventure, coauthored with Steven Best (2001)

Media and Cultural Studies: Key Works, coedited with Gigi Durham (2001)

Herbert Marcuse: Toward a Critical Theory of Society, edited (2001)

Film, Art, and Politics: An Emile de Antonio Reader, coedited with Dan Streible (2000)

Herbert Marcuse: Technology, War, and Fascism, edited (1998)

The Postmodern Turn, coauthored with Steven Best (1997)

Articulating the Global and the Local: Globalization and Cultural Studies, coedited with Ann Cvetkovich (1996)

Media Culture: Cultural Studies, Identity, and Politics between the Modern and the Postmodern (1995)

The Persian Gulf TV War (1992)

Postmodern Theory: Critical Interrogations, coauthored with Steven Best (1991)

Television and the Crisis of Democracy (1990)

Critical Theory, Marxism, and Modernity (1989)

Jean Baudrillard: From Marxism to Postmodernism and Beyond (1989)

Camera Politica: The Politics and Ideology of Contemporary Hollywood Film, coauthored with Michael Ryan (1988)

Herbert Marcuse and the Crisis of Marxism (1984)